How to Throw a Golf Club

How to Throw a Golf Club

Learn to Throw for Distance and Accuracy

by Tom Carey

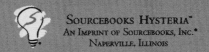

SOURCEBOOKS HYSTERIA™
AN IMPRINT OF SOURCEBOOKS, INC.®
NAPERVILLE, ILLINOIS

Published by Sourcebooks Hysteria, an imprint of Sourcebooks, Inc.
P.O. Box 4410, Naperville, Illinois 60567-4410
(630) 961-3900
Fax: (630) 961-2168
www.sourcebooks.com

Previously published as The Club Thrower's Handbook

Library of Congress Cataloging-in-Publication Data

Carey, Tom.
  How to throw a golf club / Tom Carey.
      p. cm.
    1. Golf—Humor. 2. Golf clubs (Sporting goods)—Humor. I. Title.

PN6231.G68C37 2005
818'.5402—dc22

                                                        2005025009

Printed and bound in the United States of America
RRD 10 9 8 7 6 5 4 3

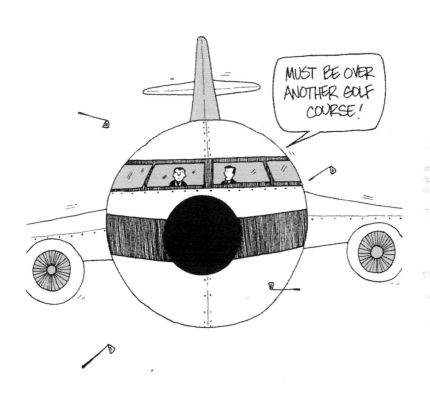

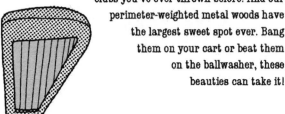

"It thrills crowds to see a guy suffer. That's why I threw clubs so often. They love to see golf get the better of someone, and I was only too happy to oblige them. At first I threw clubs because I was angry. After a while it became showmanship, plain and simple. I learned that if you helicopter those dudes by throwing them sideways instead of overhand, the shaft wouldn't break as easy. It's an art, it really is."

—"Terrible" Tommy Bolt

This book is dedicated to the **87%** of golfers who admit to having ever thrown a club.

And to the **13%** who lied about it.

Contents

A List of Our Advertisers

We are happy to recommend the following fine products and hope that you will patronize our advertisers.

Gator Bait Club Throwing Schools

Happy Feet Golf Shoes

Club Toss Golfwear

Whirlybird Golf Clubs

Lady Launcher Golf Clubs

Grip-Tite Golf Gloves

"The most exquisitely satisfying act in the world of golf is that of throwing a club. The full backswing, the delayed wrist action, the flowing follow-through, followed by that unique whirring sound, reminiscent of a passing flock of birds, are without parallel in sport."

—Henry Longhurst

CHAPTER 1

Heave 'Em and Leave 'Em: An Introduction

I love the game of golf. You can tell how much I love the game of golf because, just like the TV announcers who act as though winning the Masters is the same as curing cancer, I call it "the game of golf" instead of just "golf."

I say this loudly and I say it proudly. I have worn sherbet-colored alpaca sweaters. I have worn shirts with little penguins, crocodiles, and polo ponies on them. I have worn Sans-A-Belt slacks in colors and patterns found nowhere in nature. I have worn saddle shoes with a frilly little flap on them. More than that, I have worn ankle socks to match.

I subscribe to *Golf Magazine*, *Golf Digest*, *Golf World*, *Golf Tips*, *Golf Illustrated*, *Golf Tips Illustrated*, *World of Golf Tips Illustrated Magazine & Digest*, and *Playboy* (but only for the golf articles). My web browser has 268 bookmarks to websites that concern golf courses, golf tournaments, golf history, golf

statistics, golf vacations, and drink recipes (for after the round).

Neither rain, nor sleet, nor snow, nor gloom of night has ever kept me from my appointed round of golf, especially if I had a tee time guaranteed with a major credit card.

And, yes, it's true—I throw my clubs. I toss them like a salad, heave them like last night's Cabernet, and kick them like a set of new tires. And I'm proud of this. If you throw your clubs (and I'm sure you do; how else would you come to possess this book?), you should be proud of it, too. Far from being a shameful thing, I contend that on the contrary, club throwing is an art. It relieves stress, burns calories, builds muscle, and it keeps all the nearby players on their toes.

This book is for those golfers who have never quite been able to control their tempers. It's for those golfers whose only relief after a terrible shot comes when the offending club is soaring skyward or rattling across some parking lot, throwing sparks as it skips along.

By virtue of the guide book now in your hands, you have officially become a member in good standing of the Club Throwers of America. There are no dues to pay and no meetings to attend. I know you need every cent for new golf clubs and for higher –insurance premiums. Just having another

golfer in the brotherhood of Club Throwers is enough for me. (Though the dough I got for the book is nice, too.)

So grab the old Ping Hoofer and head on out to your favorite track. Tee it high and let it fly. And when that first tee ball does a major right-to-right on you, rear back and loft your driver after it. If it ends up on the clubhouse roof, well, so be it. Smile proudly and unapologetically at the outraged members marching across the fairway toward you and say, "I'm a Club Thrower. We heave 'em and leave 'em."

"Why am I using a new putter? Because the last one did not float too well."

—Craig Stadler

CHAPTER 2

Throwing Clubs for Distance and Accuracy

Just as there is a right way and a wrong way to *swing* a golf club, there is a right way and a wrong way to *throw* a golf club. These brief instructions are to guide you, the proud and happy Club Thrower, in the fine art of "implement levitation." After you master the basics feel free to improvise.

The Two-Handed Method

This is far and away (hmm, now there's a nice choice of words) the most popular club-heaving style among players today. But many fail to achieve the kind of distance or accuracy that is necessary for a truly "elevating" experience. The following tips will help you get the most out of every club (and tantrum) you throw.

1. Take the club back in a flat arc, parallel to the ground. A good shoulder turn is very important to get the lift you need.

2. Begin the forward swing with a quick turn of the front shoulder and step toward the target. Keeping the arms extended, release the club at about eye level. This will impart a counterclockwise spin (clockwise for you lefties) and insure maximum height and carry. Some club tossers find that a grunt or scream such as "Take that you worthless piece of scrap metal!" is helpful.

3. Follow through by stepping toward the target. Watch the flight of the club carefully and, if necessary, warn other players of the incoming missile with the traditional cry of "Hey, you guys, look out!"

The "Slam Dunk" Method

Many of the throws players use require the club to slam into something: the ground, a ball washer, the ranger, whatever. These "throws" can be dangerous because of the sudden jolt to the player's musculoskeletal system when the club contacts its target. Flying pieces of wood, steel, and flesh can also be hazardous. The following method will help you minimize physical risk and maximize the havoc you can wreak.

1. Take the club back in a smooth, single motion. As described previously, try to get a full extension of the arms.

2. Keep the elbows firm, but not locked, during the downswing and all the way

through impact. If executed properly, the offending club will bury in the ground or shatter into pieces with a satisfying snap.

CHAPTER 3

Historical Heavers: Club Throwing's Colorful Past

Golf was invented one typically dark, rainy afternoon in St. Andrews, Scotland, by Olde Tom Morris and his son, Young Tom Morris. (The Scots are notoriously unimaginative when it comes to naming their kids.) They were spending their day as usual, hanging out by Loch Ness with their cameras, waiting for the monster to appear, when a bored Young Tom absentmindedly took a swipe at a stone on the beach with his walking stick.

As fate would have it, the stone flew straight at an old, gnarled oak tree some distance away. As they walked up to the tree, Olde Tom said to his son, "I'll bet ye five bob ye kin nawt strike the tree wi' another stroke." Though the rock lay just three feet from the base of the tree, Young Tom began to shake and sweat from the pressure of the wager and, of course, he missed the short putt.

Young Tom was furious. He smashed his walking stick against the tree again and again until it broke. Then he picked up the pieces and threw them into the sea

screaming, "It's the devil's oon game we invented and I'll ne'er play it agin!"

That is how Young Tom Morris invented the yips and Olde Tom Morris invented the Nassau. And, not incidentally, the game of golf. And, of course, club throwing.

The two Scotsmen bought new sticks and were back out on the beach again the next day, swinging and swearing and throwing their clubs at nearby sheep and innocent passersby. To this day club throwing remains an integral part of the great game of golf.

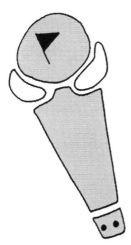

"I don't enjoy playing video golf because there is nothing to throw."

—Paul Azinger

CHAPTER 4

What's the Rule?

Bob tees off on a long par four and hits a wild slice that could be out of bounds. Naturally, he flings his driver in disgust. Unfortunately, the wayward wand caroms off a bench, snaps in two, and a piece of graphite shrapnel pierces the thigh of Bob's playing partner, Jim.

Jim collapses to the ground screaming, blood spurting from his femoral artery in a long, pulsing, crimson arc. He falls in such a way as to cover the entire teeing area. Bob is unable to re-tee within the tee box to hit his provisional ball, what with all the gushing blood and thrashing about. What is the ruling in this situation?

Rule 38-3d states that "Anytime a player has been grievously injured during play he may be declared an 'immovable obstruction.' Players may take a drop two club lengths away from the body, no closer to the hole."

Bob may elect to drop just behind or to the side of Jim and play his provisional ball.

This will be his third stroke. If he finds his first ball, of course, he may play it with no penalty.

It is considered proper etiquette to apply a tourniquet to Jim's leg with the remaining piece of his driver and a golf towel, and perhaps move Jim's body into a shady area; that is, if all this can be done without delaying play. It is also considered good form for Bob to call the paramedics at his earliest opportunity, either at the halfway house or immediately after putting out on eighteen.

In match play, Jim loses any hole he is physically unable to complete. In stroke play, he incurs a two-stroke penalty for every pint of blood spilled on the course.

If he has completed at least nine holes, Jim must report his score to the handicap committee before going to the emergency room.

"Real golfers, no matter what the provocation, never strike a caddie with the driver. The sand wedge is far more effective."

—Huxtable Pippey

CHAPTER 5

Club Tossing: An Interlude

Ah, the first tee. It is a sunny morning, bright with promise. There are eighteen beautiful, unblemished holes stretched out before you. You gaze down at the smooth, clean scorecard that could (who knows?!) in just four short hours hold evidence of a par. Or two. Maybe a birdie! Maybe (dare I say it?) you'll shoot your handicap!

You tee up a brand new ball. You take one practice swing; then another. Then a waggle or two. Or eight. A smooth, slow backswing and "pow;" you strike the ball a solid blow. It sails magnificently into the cloudless blue sky. You then watch with mounting dismay as it curves, gently at first, then violently rightward, past the clean white stakes that separate the golf course from nearby condominiums and out of bounds. The gentle tinkle of breaking glass is heard, and a distant expletive.

Still, all is not lost. You take a deep breath to relax the shoulders. You reach into your bag and pull out a fresh new twelve-dollar sleeve of balls. Calmly, you re-tee, go

through your whole pre-shot routine again, and swing. Bananaville. Then a worm burner, a couple of pop-ups, a shank, and a chilly-dip, and finally, finally, you manage to scrape one onto the front fringe.

Your first putt is thirty feet, straight uphill. You crouch behind your line. You walk all around it. You plumb bob it. You step up and give it a good rap. And you leave it short by at least five feet. You pause to gather your thoughts.

One of your playing partners clears his throat and says quietly, "You're still away."

Shaken from your reverie, you step up again. Firmly then, you think to yourself, firmly; to the back of the cup. You make what you know is a solid stroke. The ball rolls two feet past the cup.

As you step up to tap it in, it seems your partners have all contracted a mysterious case of lockjaw. Surely they don't expect you to putt this tiny thing? After such a hideous beginning they're not going to concede you a two-foot putt? You've played together for years. You've attended the weddings, christenings, and birthdays of their children. They know what the game of golf means to you. But there is no sound. None, save the gentle lowing of a herd of cows in a nearby pasture. "Snowman, snowman, snowman," seems to be their mournful refrain.

"Okay," you think. "Fine. This is not a problem." You line up your two-footer as carefully as you would any putt. Then you carefully and confidently stroke the ball and watch in horror as it veers off a spike mark, hits the lip, does a 360 and pops out just inches from where it started.

Somehow, you remain calm. You employ the mental imaging techniques you read about in a recent magazine article about golf psychology. You are "in the moment." Your heart is pure. You are close to achieving a true Zen experience.

And then, one of your partners says it.

"That one's good."

That's what does it, really. That smug,

condescending, pitying tone of voice. The rage in you begins to build. Your peaceful state of mind crumbles before the tidal wave of black bile roaring through your veins. The sound of the entire world is obliterated by the voice in your head screaming that you just began your round of golf by desecrating the scorecard with a brutal, hideous, soul-destroying ten.

You look down at the putter in your hands. And it is clear what you must do. You rear back and, as your playing partners scramble for the safety of the bushes, golf cart, and sand bunker, you heave that sucker. It flies high and far, elegantly and majestically, end-over-end and out of bounds. It bounces in the

nearby road with a satisfying clank and disappears beneath the wheels of a passing bus.

You relax. As your playing partners come out from under cover, you stroll casually to the next tee thinking, "Hell, I'll probably putt better with my two-iron anyway."

"Sometimes the game of golf is just too difficult to endure with a golf club in your hands."

—Bobby Jones

CHAPTER 6

On the Beach

So many players are intimidated when faced with a difficult sand shot. Chances are they'll take two or three tries before throwing the ball out in disgust. A perfect opportunity to throw a club? You bet. However, some precautions must be taken to insure a satisfying club-throwing experience when you're "on the beach."

Equipment

If you don't have a sand wedge, get one. This handy club is specially lofted, flanged, and weighted to fly perfectly, end-over-end when tossed from a bunker. If you prefer to bury it up to the grip with a resounding overhead smash, it will sink deeply into the sand with a satisfying THUNK.

It is very important to have a pair of good golf shoes when throwing clubs from the sand. Spiked or spikeless, these shoes will allow you to get solid footing where you otherwise might slip.

To do your best in the sand, follow these tips!

1. Take a wider stance than normal with feet, hips, knees, and shoulders aimed well left of the target.

2. Draw the club back as usual, remembering to keep your lower body "quiet."

3. As you bring the club forward to release it, stride toward your target. Following through with a snap of the wrist will ensure maximum height and club flight. Your sand wedge should bury wherever it lands.

Yes, the sand can be intimidating, but with practice and the right equipment you should be able to heave a club just as far from the sand as you can from a nice lie in the fairway.

"Never break your putter and your driver in the same round or you're dead."

—"Terrible" Tommy Bolt

CHAPTER 7
Club Throwing
Q & A

Q. Isn't throwing your club an unsafe thing to do?

A. Not if it's done properly! Novice club throwers can cause lots of damage to the course and to their playing partners, but for those heavers who have been around awhile it's safety first! The first rule of club throwing is, always throw your club forward! You'll get a clear look at club line of flight, be able to warn any players who might be in danger, and you'll be able to pick the club up as you walk by. And, as club-throwing patron saint "Terrible" Tommy Bolt has said, "if you toss a club backwards you'll just have to run back to get it."

Also, it's important to warm up thoroughly before you throw any clubs to avoid back strain and pulled muscles. (See the chapter entitled Let's Work Out!)

Q. I've never thrown a club before. How do I get started on the right foot?

A. Always start your club throwing with some practice time at the range. More and more driving ranges these days offer club-throwing areas where you can rent a bag of clubs (usually about five dollars for a large bag) and practice heaving them.

Warm up with a few short throws. Toss a couple of wedges and putters. Then as your muscles begin to loosen up, begin to throw the longer and heavier clubs working your way up gradually to the woods.

After you get the hang of it you may want to add some cursing and swearing. Veteran club tossers find that a few well-chosen screams add immeasurably to the enjoyment they get when throwing clubs.

Q. Can women throw clubs as well as men?

A. Certainly! Women may not be able to heave clubs as far as men, of course, but what they lack in upper-body strength they can make up for in style and grace. Many a wife has put her husband to shame by following one of his wild and wobbly heaves with a picture-perfect, end-over-end toss into a lateral hazard. You go girl!

Q. How soon should I have my kids start throwing their golf clubs?

A. At Club Throwers of America it's our belief that children are the bearers of the club-throwing torch. The future of club tossing in this nation is in our golfing youth. If your kids are

old enough to play, they're old enough to throw clubs. Kids have an advantage over us old folks in that many of them have yet to develop good habits and manners. Throwing clubs in anger and having tantrums in public comes naturally to most kids, and you'll probably find that they respond enthusiastically to your efforts to guide them in our wonderful pastime.

Q. Don't many golf courses frown on club throwing?

A. Sadly, it's true that many clubs still discourage the healthy release of anger that comes from lofting a club or two skyward. But we've made great strides in recent years and we hope that soon every golf course will be open to the proud and happy club thrower.

"Golf appeals to the idiot in us and the child."

—John Updike

CHAPTER 8

Let's Work Out!

Club throwing, like any strenuous activity, requires that you be in good shape to perform at your peak. With that in mind, we have created an exercise program that combines the principles of muscle development and aerobic fitness, especially for the club thrower who wishes to increase his enjoyment of the sport.

Do this workout every other day and you'll soon see your clubs reach new heights and distances. You may be tempted to skip workouts at times. The excuses are endless: it takes too much time, you don't have any place to do it, your wife has already threatened to leave you if you break anything else in the house with a golf club, etc.

But remember, the short time you spend getting and staying in shape will pay off ten-fold on the course. So stick to it!

The Two-Iron Twist

1. Begin this warm-up exercise with a two-iron held high over your head. Twist slowly to the left, keeping arms fully extended.

2. Make about a 90-degree turn. Then twist back to your start position and continue until you reach about a 90-degree turn to the right.

Do twelve reps, rest one minute, then do twelve more.

The Rail Splitter

Just like old Honest Abe, you'll want to wield your club like an axe at times. This exercise will work the muscles you'll need.

1. Start with the club head on the ground, arms extended in front of you. Draw the club back directly over your head, as far as you can.

2. Bring your club back overhead and to your starting position.

Do twelve reps, rest one minute, do twelve reps again.

The Hammer Throw

1. Begin this exercise in the same position as "The Rail Splitter." Spin slowly in a circle, again holding the club at a full arm's length.

2. Allow centrifugal force to raise the club up to about eye level as you spin faster and faster.

Do this exercise for five minutes or until you fall down.

The O.B. Hop

This is one you can do on the course while waiting for the other members in your group to hit. It's great aerobically and it will come in handy when sneaking over the out-of-bounds fence to find wayward clubs.

1. Grasp the top of a fence rail. Using your hands for balance, throw both legs over to the other side.
2. Repeat this action in reverse.

Do 3 sets of 10 reps each.

The Scythe

Great for the man who wants to carve out
his own space.

1. Swing club side to side extending as
   far each way as you can.

"If you are going to throw a club, it is important to throw it ahead of you, down the fairway, so you do not waste energy going back to pick it up."

—"Terrible" Tommy Bolt

CHAPTER 9
Ante Up!

For many players the enjoyment of a round of golf, and the ensuing mayhem created by flying clubs, is heightened by a bit of wagering. Betting in golf is a long-standing tradition among players, and betting on club tossing is fast becoming as fashionable and as fun as betting on the score.

Following are a few betting games that will increase your enjoyment of the game, focus your concentration, hone your competitive edge, and keep your club-throwing skills sharp.

The Scotch Game

This is a partner game in which players score points throwing their clubs for distance and accuracy. A typical match might have six points available on each hole; two for the most throws, two for the longest heaves, and two for whoever imbeds his club in the green closest to the pin.

The Nassau

This traditional bet awards a set amount of money for most club throws on the front nine, most on the back nine, and most for the overall eighteen. There are numerous variations on the Nassau and players may include rules about how often they may "press," or double the bet, and what kind of "presses" are permitted.

One favorite twist on this game is the "flying press" in which players are allowed to double the bet while the club is in the air, and may offer side bets on where it will land, how many pieces it will break into, whether it will cause property damage, and on the total dollar amount of that damage.

Some players play "The Lawsuit" game and place wagers on the amount of damages an injured golfer can collect from a club thrower, or how much he'll settle for out of court. The variations are endless.

The Horse Race

This is an individual game in which an unlimited number of players start at the first hole and play until they throw a club. Players who throw a club must drop out and the last player left collects all the loot. It's sort of like golf course musical chairs.

The Skins Game

In this game, each hole is worth a set amount and players play as individuals against the other members of the group. If two players tie on a hole, everyone ties the hole and the skin carries over to the next hole. For example, if player A throws three clubs on a hole and no one else throws a

club more than twice, player A wins the hole. However, if player A throws two clubs and player B throws two clubs, the hole is tied and the skin carries over, even if players C and D don't throw any clubs at all.

CHAPTER 10

Getting Really Teed Off!

Throwing that first club of the day can really set the tone for your round. If, after your first miserable, pathetic attempt at a golf swing, which sends your first tee ball trickling sadly off the cart path by the ladies' tee, you stride confidently forward and launch your driver straight down the fairway, you can then march down the middle and proudly scoop up what's left of your club before continuing play, now comfortable in the knowledge that you've gotten off on the right foot. If your first toss is a shaky one that barely clears the front of the tee box, you may spend the rest of the round trying to recover your equilibrium.

The key to getting off to a proper club-throwing start is a good, solid twenty-minute warm-up session. Start by throwing a few putters around. It gets the blood pumping! Move to the chipping and pitching area and toss a few wedges around there, scattering those players foolishly practicing there. Throw some clubs from the practice sand

trap if your driving range has one. Then move to the range itself and try some full throws, first with the short irons and then working your way up to the woods.

After you're warm and loose and feel like nothing can stand in the way of you and club-throwing greatness, stroll confidently to the first tee. Bang your five-iron on the door of the Port-A-Potty as you march by. Sneer at the starter as he reads his little spiel about fast play and good sportsmanship. Kick the tee markers just for fun. Then send your driver where that sucker was meant to go.

This will get you off on the right foot every time!

"Here's irony for you: The driver goes the shortest distance when you throw it. The putter flies farthest, followed by the sand wedge."

—"Terrible" Tommy Bolt

CHAPTER 11

The Twenty Basic Club Throws

To be a truly successful club thrower you must master the Twenty Basic Club Throws. Each of these is described and illustrated in the following pages. Make these tosses part of your regular practice and soon you'll be the envy of all your playing partners. In addition, you'll have the basis for inventing and perfecting your own club throws and developing your own unique club-throwing style.

Each of the basic tosses is shown here with a little club-tossing poem that you should memorize. This is a mnemonic device (like Every Good Boy Does Fine, for instance), which will help you to remember, in the heat of your club throwing passion, the correct throw for each situation that you find yourself in.

Once you have committed these to memory you'll be on your way to a new and much more fulfilling club-throwing career!

The Whirlybird

It soars so gently through the air,
Like a chopper in the blue,
You fling your club with style and flair,
Because you are a chopper, too.

This is the classic toss. Use the basic method as described in Chapter 2. This toss is appropriate in almost all club-throwing situations, especially on the first and tenth tee when you'll have spectators and will want to look your best.

The Rainmaker

Cumulus clouds and thunderheads,
May have a silver lining,
But go to any nineteenth hole,
And you'll hear some real whining.

Again, this is a classic. Start with the club-head on the ground, arms extended in front of you. Squat until your thighs are approximately parallel to the ground. Then spring upward and thrust your club skyward. Remember to follow through completely. And to duck!

Fling!

70

The Tree Coil

A putter you will oft times see,

Stuck high up in a leafy tree,

But strange as though I've always found it,

You'll sometimes see one wrapped around it.

This "toss" is especially good when you've just tried a miracle shot you had no business trying and your ball has hit a tree and has actually gone deeper into the woods than it was before. Get a full shoulder turn and hit the tree about halfway up the shaft and it should bend around the trunk nicely. Or, it could shatter into a dozen pieces, and that's nice, too. Not recommended when the temperature is below 55 degrees.

The Scraper

Ruin in a fit of rage,
A club on which for years you've doted,
And later you may rue the fact,
That golf clubs are not Teflon coated.

Sometimes you'll just want to drag that bad boy on the ground for a while. This can be fun because there are so many interesting surfaces on and around the golf course available to do damage to your golf clubs. Try the easy access cart path for starters, the sidewalk by the clubhouse, or the gravel parking lot. If you're really ticked off, you can tie one to the bumper of your car for the ride home.

HAHAHA HA HA

SKIP   SCRAPE   SKRATCH   SKIP

The Tee Plant

Like Johnny with his apple seeds,
You pound your tees in everywhere,
Perhaps you'll drive one in so deep,
That soon a tee tree will grow there.

Sometimes, just for a change of pace, you'll want to take your anger out on something other than your clubs. One of the most satisfying ways to vent your spleen is to pound your tee into the turf until it disappears. There are tees now available on the market made of fertilizer that are actually good for the grass. Just the excuse you need to use this club "throw."

The Javelin Toss

Before you heave a club this way,
Warm up first and do your stretching,
You'd rather do the javelin throw,
Than try to do the javelin catching.

Good form is the key to this stylish toss. Imagine yourself as an Olympic decathlete as you get your running start. After about a twenty or thirty yard sprint, turn sideways holding your club like a javelin, grip forward. Plant your front foot and fling the club up and out using hips, shoulders, and legs for power. With practice you'll be able to stick a two-iron in the turf like a headhunter's spear.

The Oil Well

Four tries and still you're in the sand,

Your teeth may grind, your blood may boil,

But look upon the brighter side,

You're very close to striking oil!

The key here is to use your sand wedge to get as much sand as you can out of the bunker. Happily, this club is made for exactly that, with a high degree of loft and a wide flange. A determined club thrower can empty an average-sized greenside bunker in ten minutes flat.

The Hankie Drop

Coquettishly you drop your club,
Though you'd rather let it fly,
You're certainly a gentleman,
When the ranger is nearby.

Sadly, many golf courses still frown on club tossing. Some places will even ask you to leave if you attempt to practice this fine art. Should you find yourself at one of these behind-the-times tracks you may have to be content with this genteel little toss. Until the ranger takes off anyway.

THONK

The Spike

Football players celebrate,

When they go for six,

They slam the ball down just the way

You slam your useless sticks.

Be as creative as you like on this one! Go behind the back, between the legs, or slam-dunk a club over a nearby tree. Throw in a little touchdown dance.

The Over-The-Shoulder

Casually you toss your club,
But forget to look behind you,
A partner, though, may find a way,
To painfully remind you.

When going for club throwing "style" points
it can be tempting to fling one over your
shoulder without looking. Unfortunately, this
little habit can result in injuries and lawsuits.
So look before you heave!

HOW TO THROW A GOLF CLUB

The Ubangi Stomp

The tantrums that you often throw,
Are like an ancient tribal dance,
You lack the face paint and the feathers,
But at least you have the pants.

Ugly pants have always had a place in the game of golf, and they can really enhance your enjoyment of this little tantrum. When you miss a little putt it's fun to high step around the hole in agony, screaming an unintelligible string of curses and gibberish in a high, wailing voice. This has the added benefit of tearing up the green around the hole for the people in your group who still have to putt out.

The Twist

You three putt for the seventh time,
Will this never stop?
Your putter's like an ice cold beer,
With a twist-off top.

Three (and four and five) putting is a great reason to mangle your equipment. Since most club throwers have well-developed wrists and forearms from those twist-off beer caps, popping a putter head or two should be no problem.

The Roof Shot

The condo owner won't return,
The putter he found on his roof,
Golf is not the game you play,
The game you play is goof.

During your club-throwing career you'll find that it's tempting to fire a club or two. There is something undeniably pleasing about a well-thrown golf club hurtling over a fence and disappearing. The resulting crash and cry of surprise and pain can be amusing too.

The Trespasser

You climbed the fence in search of clubs,

You tossed into the morning fog,

You never saw that backyard sign,

The one that said, "Beware of Dog."

Lots of people who bought golf course property for the peace and quiet have found themselves living under siege. They may be less than understanding about your club throwing needs. In this case it's best to let sleeping dogs lie.

The Swashbuckler

Galahad and knights of old,
Were gallant swordsmen just like you,
Woe unto a laughing looper,
You might run that sucker through.

Many caddies have developed a less-than-reverent attitude toward club throwers. It is important to keep these youngsters in line for your sake and for your club-throwing brothers who may have to deal with the insolent wretches later.

HOW TO THROW A GOLF CLUB

The Repeater

Thrice you try a three-foot putt,

For par, and thrice you rim it,

Too bad the rules of golf enforce,

A strict fourteen-club limit.

As you develop your club heaving you'll want to add speed to your arsenal of skills to go along with distance and accuracy. Practice at the range and see how fast you can empty a bag of golf clubs. Some advanced club tossers will throw clubs with both hands!

The Swizzle Stick

The poolside guest may be upset,
He may cause quite a stink,
If that club you lofted came,
To rest within his drink.

Target tossing can be loads of fun. And golf course targets are plentiful, especially along the ninth and eighteenth holes. Firing a putter into the pool, clubhouse, or tennis courts can bring true club heaving pleasure, as well as a hefty bill for damages. But that's the price you pay for having so darn much fun.

The Caddie-Killer

Heavy bags and flying clubs,
Make jocking less than super,
They're the hazards that make up,
The life of every looper.

Hey, these kids get paid well. They need to be on their toes! If you should accidentally spear a slow-moving caddy with a flying four wood it's their problem. Club throwing etiquette does require that you double the tip for any caddy who ends up needing emergency room treatment.

The Speed Bump

Tossing one's clubs,
One by one is an art,
But to efficiently wreck them,
You must use a cart.

Sometimes you just want to smash all your clubs to pieces and go to the bar. That's why it's important to practice this key club "toss." Don't just run your bag over. Back your cart up and get a good head of steam. Tip one of the clubhouse boys to get you one of the souped up carts they use to tear around the course at night when no one else is around.

The Ice Fisher

Into the blust'ry winter chill,
The golfer treks undaunted,
Tho his presence on the ice,
May oft times be unwanted.

As a dedicated club thrower you must practice your art even in very difficult conditions. Throw your clubs in the spring. Throw them in the summer, fall, and winter, too. Throw them at the public course and throw them when invited to the private country club. Throw them in the rain, the sleet, the snow, and in the hot sunshine. Throw them whenever and wherever the mood strikes you, but, whatever you do...THROW THEM!

"He enjoys that perfect peace, that peace beyond all understanding, which comes at its maximum only to the man who has given up golf."

—P. G. Wodehouse

CHAPTER 12

You Know You're a Club Thrower If...

1. The club repair guy at your local course names his first child after you.
2. Your regular caddy wears a catcher's mask and chest protector.
3. When you reach into your bag to select a club your playing partners dive for cover.
4. You have learned to putt with every other club in the bag.

5. Your local course now requires that you leave a security deposit along with your green fees.

6. Your homeowners insurance company has you in your own separate risk pool.

7. You are deluged with business cards from personal injury attorneys each time you play.

8. You have developed carpal tunnel syndrome from your repetitive throwing motion.

9. You carry duct tape and crazy glue in your bag.

10. Like Michael Jordan, your nickname is also "Air."

About the Author

Tom Carey is a writer and illustrator from Chicago who plays golf all the time and only throws a club if it really, really deserves it.